Save A Young Adult

17 SECRETS TO END Tendencies To ANXIETY & DEPRESSION

Author Ana Lennyr,

Premier Life Strategist &

Founder of the AntiDepression Institute

www.analennyr.com

ISBN: 979-8-218-58817-5

First Edition: February, 2025

United States of America

Dedication

I dedicate this book to Doina (my mother), Daniel (my son), and Jonathan D. who guided me in life to become a premier life strategist and ultimately the Founder of the AntiDepression Institute.

Prayer

'May this book find its way to the ones who are looking for guidance'

Disclaimer

This book is designed to provide information and motivation to our readers, and in no way should it be used as a substitute for consultation with a healthcare professional. This book is not meant to be used and shall not be used to diagnose or treat any medical or psychological condition. For diagnosis or treatment of any medical or psychological problem, consult your physician or qualified mental health professional, and you should see the services of a competent professional before beginning any improvement or health program.

The content of this book is the sole expression and opinion of its author, with the understanding that the author is not engaged in rendering any type of medical, psychological, legal, or any other kind of professional advice. You should not consider educational material herein to be a practice of medicine, psychotherapy, or any healthcare, or to replace consultation with a physician, other medical practitioner, or psychotherapist. The author is providing you with information so that you can choose, at your own risk, to act on that information.

While best efforts have been used in preparing this book, the author makes no representations, warranties, or guarantees of any kind assumes no liabilities of any kind concerning the accuracy or completeness of the content and specifically disclaims any implied warranties of merchantability or health or fitness or use for a particular purpose.

The author assumes no responsibility and shall not be held liable or responsible to any person or entity for any errors or omissions, or for injuries, losses, physical, medical, psychological, emotional, financial, or commercial damages, including, but not limited to, special, incidental, consequential or other damages, or alleged to have been caused, directly or indirectly, by information or programs contained herein.

The author is not responsible for any specific needs that may require medical or psychological supervision and is not liable for any damages or negative consequences from any treatment, action, application, or preparation, to any person reading or following information in this book.

References are provided for informational purposes only and do not constitute endorsement of any website or other sources.

Readers should be aware that the website listed in this book may change.

The stories, names, and identities of the people in the book have been extensively disguised so that any resemblance to any person, living or dead, is coincidental. Most of the cases represent composites of many patients with similar problems. The intention is to protect patient confidentiality while preserving the spirit of the work.

Our views and rights are the same: You are responsible for your own choices, actions, and results.

Your Gift

Even though this book is designed to be extremely efficient for young adults, parents, educators, and community leaders, it may not have all the answers you might be seeking. This is why many people hire coaches and mentors to see things from a different perspective, finding shortcuts and practical ways to implement their ideas faster, better, and more effectively.

Along with this book, I have decided to give you access to a free answer to any question you may have about any challenge in life you might be struggling with.

I would suggest using your gift in addition to his book to never encounter suffering in your life.

Get your free answer at:

www.mychallengeis.org

Anonymous

"I was planning not to live like this anymore. I decided ...after my shift was ending. You came in to buy sour cream and you were so happy. I couldn't believe it.

Then you looked into my eyes and realized how sad I was. Part of me was afraid you knew what I was about to do. Part of me wanted you to know.

You smiled, gave me your business card, and told me to call you.

I was intrigued so I looked you up.

I did call you and I became your client.

I never knew that it was so simple to change my life.

Thank you for finding me."

How Can YOU Save a Young Adult?

YOU CAN save a young adult by preparing them correctly for a real life and guiding them to end tendencies to anxiety and depression - a responsibility we all must share.

The 17 'secrets' shared in this book answer the major questions that young adults have in our society today.

You can choose to:

- Give this book to someone who you feel needs it (young adult or their parent) or at least recommend it;
- Leave us an honest review on Amazon (or any other platform) if you found any value in this book so others can also find value;
- Contact us and join our mission:

Save A Young Adult at:

www.saveayoungadult.com

About this book…

The 'secrets' shared in this book are the ones our young adults are seeking, but can't find because they don't know the right questions to ask.

If I would've known these 17 life secrets, I could've dodged 27 years of depression. If my mom, a top-notch teacher, who battled alcoholism, would've known these 'secrets', her life would've turned out differently. No one passed these insights to me, and I found myself in the dark, nearly harming my child who displayed tendencies of anxiety and depression at the age of 8.

This book comes from my failures as a parent and teacher, and my successes and experiences as a life strategist at the AntiDepression Institute.

With every single secret, I will show you how this vital knowledge can seriously save young adults and their families, and how not knowing it could affect them well into their late 30s.

As educators, parents, and mentors, we hold the key to arming our children with the tools and skills to stop unnecessary suffering and pave the way for a brighter tomorrow. We have to safeguard our young adults and prepare them for life appropriately.

How Can This Book Help a Young Adult?

This book contains 17 universal secrets to GUIDE YOUNG ADULTS IN LIFE, ages 12 to 35. I wish I had known these secrets as a young adult so I could find my purpose in life sooner and not wander the world in darkness and suffering while hurting myself and my son.

These 17 True Secrets of Life (as I call them) can easily help any young adult to begin to find their identity, deal with emotional instability, and discover their purpose in life. The main goal is to be able to find their way to live their "Vera Vita" or **TRUE LIFE** (an acronym for **T**rust, **R**espect, **U**nderstanding, **E**volving, and **L**ive **I**ncredibly **F**ulfilling **E**veryday).

For any young adult, these 17 secrets can allow them to STOP suffering and START living a True Life.

Our Mission

For anyone suffering from anxiety or depressive tendencies, their life looks like a bad dream that they can't wake up from. Once they overcome these tendencies, they realize that everything they know about life is very different.

Our entire mission at the AntiDepression Institute is to guide teenagers and adults to prevent and overcome suffering based on LIFE STRATEGY, a new and holistic approach to mental health, complementary to other traditional methods.

Our goals include:

- Giving a young adult the answers about the life they are seeking (17 of them included in this book);
- **Showing them that suffering is not necessary in life and there are ways to resolve it if this happens;**
- Teaching them how to master relationships, emotional balance, and mental strength so they will never be trapped in challenges.

How To Use This Book as A Parent?

By the time you get this book, your young adult might not listen to you. If they do, it's easy, just let them read it. If they refuse everything that is coming from you, that is because they're angry, upset, and lost, just like I was once.

The best way to help them is actually enrolling them in our program **How Life Truly Works** (including 10 extra secrets at www.howlifetrulyworks.org), designed specifically for overcoming the following challenges that parents are usually struggling with:

- **To boost effectiveness, daily program videos are sent to both your cell phone and your child's cell phone for 27 days. This helps your child be more receptive and allows them to listen at their convenience.**
- You'll learn how to start conversations with your child and determine what they understand and what they don't. This is crucial, as missing key life insights can hinder their self-discovery and emotional stability.
- **The program aims to strengthen your bond with your child, foster open communication, and shield them from negative external influences like social media or toxic individuals.**

How To Use This Book as A Young Adult?

When the student is ready, the teacher appears

Consider this book as a fundamental step for getting you prepared for life. Don't read it all at once. Read one secret every day, so you can process every secret and remember it when a challenge occurs.

If it's easier for you to watch videos, consider the program **How Life Truly Works** with 27 secrets (10 extra secrets) at: www.howlifetrulyworks.org

If you are over 19 and you encounter a challenge that this book does not resolve, don't keep suffering, use the FREE gift associated with a book at: www.mychallengeis.org

Remember this:

SUFFERING IS NOT NECESSARY IN LIFE

STAY OPEN-MINDED

Your answers will come when you are ready to hear them.

TIP – The answers will come when ANGER & ANXIETY no longer BLINDS YOU.

How To Use This Book as An Educator or Community Leader?

As educators and community leaders, our fundamental mission is to influence the lives of young adults positively. Unfortunately, a significant number of them are grappling with tendencies of anxiety, depression, anger, or low self-esteem in today's challenging world. The busy schedules of parents, the imperfect models of values from friends and families, and the potential hazards presented by social media further increase their struggles.

The 17 secrets of this book show us how to navigate these obstacles and instill valuable life lessons that can empower the youth to thrive in a complex and demanding society. The ultimate purpose is to unlock the potential of every young adult, to make a lasting difference in the lives of the next generation.

At AntiDepression Institute we are available for lectures, workshops, and licensing of our programs.

You can also join our mission:

Save A Young Adult at:

www.saveayoungadult.com

ALEX

"So why did you bring me into this world? Misery loves company or did you just want me to suffer?"

Alex only 13 years old, asked his father this question. His father, who had just become one of my clients, was taken aback and didn't know what to say. Panicked, he called me.

"I think I messed up," he admitted nervously.

"What happened?" I asked, trying to calm him down.

"He overheard me telling someone that life is suffering."

"Alright, here's what we'll do," I replied. "I'm going to text you exactly what to say to him. Don't try to wing it. Just read it exactly as I send it."

The entire message can be found at Marian's story.

Secret #1

The Purpose of Life

If you don't know the general purpose of life, how can you find your personal purpose? I remember being young and trying to read books to find reasons to live, eager to understand why we exist, especially why unhappy people exist. Nowadays, social media can easily have negative effects, especially when a child is searching for answers to this big question.

Some people say it takes a lifetime to find out, but here's the simple truth:

The purpose of life is to grow and expand

When you stop growing and expanding, you start to wither from within, and that's when suffering takes over. Once suffering takes hold, it's hard to escape because you tend to gravitate towards it. It's crucial to either avoid suffering or recognize it immediately when it occurs so you can turn things around as soon as possible.

MARIAN

"Is it normal to feel lost at 19?"

"I'm 19, and honestly, I'm clueless about my life's purpose. I feel completely lost. I don't even know which way to turn. Shouldn't I have some idea of what I want to do or who I want to become by now? How do people figure out their purpose in life? And how can I even grasp the true meaning of living?"

"***Life is a series of lessons and tests. Failing a test leads to suffering, or to tendencies toward anxiety and depression creeping in. That's a sign the lesson hasn't been mastered. When you finally understand the lesson and pass the test, the suffering vanishes. But it's just until the next lesson and next test come around,*** " I repeated the same answer I gave Alex in the text message.

Secret #2

Finding Your Own Purpose in Life

Discovering your purpose in life ***will be shaped by the mix of experiences and skills*** you gather along the way. That's why it's crucial to explore and grow in various aspects because these experiences and skills act as guiding lights toward your true calling. Expecting to have life all figured out at 19 with limited experiences and skills is a bit unrealistic. Your purpose tends to unveil itself later in life.

However, here's the tricky part. ***Your true purpose remains hidden as long as you cling to any lingering suffering.*** While you're weighed down by suffering, only a temporary purpose may surface. It's only when you shed those old suffering patterns that your real purpose emerges. ***Removing suffering is a vital test you must pass to reach your true calling.***

SANDRA

"I know all of this,"

Sandra insisted, her voice tinged with frustration. At 33, she was a single mother of two, struggling with alcoholism and still living at her parents' home.

"I've seen all your videos. I understand all of it. But my sister is still trying to take my children for days and even weeks."

"She's trying to protect them," I said gently but firmly. ***An alcoholic mother can unconsciously raise depressed children. As adults, those kids can become workaholics, attract narcissistic partners, and eventually raise their own children in an environment of depressive tendencies.*** Your sister knows all this. She is giving you space and time to focus on yourself, to straighten things out before it affects your kids even more."

Secret #3

What We Don't Know

We don't like to admit that there are things we don't know. Admitting our lack of knowledge can be challenging, as it often serves as a form of self-protection.

There are three categories of things we don't know:

1. ***Things we don't care about***, like how rockets are built or how electricity works.

2. ***Things we don't know that we don't know***. Things we don't know even exist, like different ways to handle life challenges, relationships, mental or emotional struggles. We don't know these things because no one taught us, so our brain usually dismisses them. (This is what we teach at AntiDepression Institute)

3. ***Things we think we know, but we know them partially and not completely***. This is the most dangerous category especially when overlapping with the 2nd category.

LAURA

"I just don't get how people can genuinely be happy or live an easy life,

Laura confessed at age 26, a hint of frustration in her voice.

"I had and I still have such a hard life. I'm sure others have hard lives too. Maybe they are some people who are just lucky, or maybe they're pretending and are secretly unhappy inside. The only happy people I see are actors in movies, and they're just acting. So, it's just another lie."

"So, let me guess," I replied. ***"You think your suffering comes from the tough life you've had, right? If your life had been easier, you wouldn't feel depressed or unhappy, is that correct?"*** It was the same perspective I had once.

Secret #4

Hard Life versus Easy Life

I'm going to focus on what people with an easy life understand, sometimes without even realizing it, compared to those who have a tough life.

People who struggle often think they know exactly why they're suffering and believe it's okay to suffer because everyone else is suffering too, just hiding it in different ways. They don't see that **what they actually know best is how to suffer,** and they're unaware of how to escape it, or that there's a world beyond suffering. It's hard for them to accept change.

On the other hand, ***people with easier lives recognize that there are things they don't know that they don't know.*** When they face a challenge, they explore this area to find answers. Once they find these solutions, they can easily grow, adapt, and handle whatever challenges arise.

DAVID

"I do a lot for my personal development,"

David, age 31, said enthusiastically.

"I attend all kinds of leadership conferences because I want to be one of the top leaders in my government agency."

"That's great," I replied. "Would you like to share a bit about your personal life?"

"Well... you know," David hesitated, "Things haven't been great for the last 4 years. We're staying together for our child… It's a difficult situation... It's complicated... but… I guess it is what it is."

"I see," I said thoughtfully. "***So, you want to be a top leader in your agency, but you haven't figured out how to be a leader in your own family over the last 4 years.*** I can help you with that."

Secret #5

Being Respected

Earning respect starts with you and within your family. Think about it like a test: if you don't respect yourself, or you don't have respect inside your family, how can you expect others outside your home to respect you?

There are many leadership programs out there, but ***real leaders come from self-confidence, self-respect, and a clear understanding of what they want and how to get it.*** You can try to fake it in a leadership role, but it will fall apart if you don't manage to respect and be respected by your family.

Whether or not you agree with your family members, you need to figure out how to respect yourself and those around you, and how to earn their respect. Without that, you'll struggle to gain respect outside your household.

Consider our program: *Become Mentally Strong*

ADRIAN

"I don't want to go to high school,"

The 15-year-old Mathew declared. Coming from a highly educated family with two university degrees, his mom called me immediately.

"So why don't you want to go to school?" I asked.

"First of all, the kids are stupid, and the teachers don't teach me anything useful for real life. School's a total waste of time," he said.

"How about I show you an easy way to understand how kids are thinking so you can play a really nice game with them, and... ***I will teach you things about real life and how it works,*** including how to get along with teachers? And it will only take a few minutes a day." I negotiated with him.

Secret #6

The Best Advice

The best advice I've received from really successful and influential people—those who have made billions or become top actors and singers—is to ***INVEST IN YOURSELF.*** Everything else can be taken away, but what you learn stays with you.

Investing in yourself doesn't have to be traditional. You can tailor it to fit your needs and goals. For example, young adults don't always see the immediate purpose of school. Consider school as a base or a foundation. Stronger and deeper the foundation is – more YOU can build on top. Many expect school to be everything they need in life, when actually school is just ONE TOOL (out of many) TO GET EVERY SINGLE THING YOU WANT IN LIFE.

The entire life is a school, with lessons and tests.

More you know and faster you pass the tests - happier you are.

What's crucial when investing in yourself is **knowing who you are**. This is an accelerated generation that wants all the answers at once. As educators and parents, it's our responsibility to offer them all the secrets.

ROBERT

"I'm lost on where to seek relationship advice."

"I went through a major heartbreak a couple of years back, and it still feels fresh because I can't seem to find the right partner.

My friends offer advice, but they're dealing with their own relationship issues.

My parents have been divorced for a while and are currently single.

So, where can I find better guidance on relationships?" - Robert, 23.

Consider our program: True Love Secrets.

Secret #7

Receiving Advice

Often, we don't realize that we're taking advice from the ones who haven't experienced the same problem they are trying to solve. Let's be honest: if I hadn't had the life experience I did and hadn't seen how hard it is to get out of suffering, how could I have ever understood what teens and adults need to learn today to escape suffering in life?

When seeking advice, we should turn to people who have achieved what we want to accomplish. Too often, we get misled by appearances, degrees, fashion, or what sounds appealing, without seeing if there's real substance behind it. By making these mistakes, over time, we end up ignoring even good advice because we lose trust in our gut instincts and people's sincerity.

MONICA

"I don't get how some people manage to overcome suffering," Monica, 29, admitted.

"I've tried everything—seeing different counselors, meditation, herbs, diets. But it keeps coming back every few months. Not everyone can beat it, so I feel like I'm stuck dealing with it."

"Did anyone assist you in overcoming these challenges?" I asked

"No, I tried everything by myself, I just followed my heart," she explained.

"***But your heart only knows pain, so unconsciously it leads you back to suffering, regardless of your efforts. That's why finding the right mentor is essential to guide you out of this,***" I explained.

Secret #8

Most Dangerous Mind Trap

One of the most dangerous traps I've seen, both in my work and from personal experience, is using the phrase ***"I cannot."*** Everyone faces failures, and often many failures come before success. But saying "I cannot" stops you from trying before you even begin.

There is always a way. There are many ways to tackle the same challenge or problem, but you need to be open-minded and remove "I cannot" from your belief system.

If someone else has done it before, you can too.

If no one has, you have the chance to be the first.

Anything else is just an excuse. "I cannot" is the first and most dangerous of the 17 mind traps that keep people from moving forward in their lives and from finding their true potential.

Consider our program:

The 17 Mind Traps Keeping Us In Suffering

DIANA

"I called you because I'm worried about my daughter Diana, 16 years old," her mom said.

"She seems uncomfortable going to school because she feels judged by other kids, and even by teachers.

I keep telling her that what others think doesn't matter, but it's like she's not listening.

How can I help her understand that peoples' opinions are about them, not about her?"

Secret #9

People's Role in Your Life

We can't ignore that people's opinions matter, but we need to know when they are important and when they aren't.

Imagine you're writing an essay and two people critique it. The first person doesn't know much about writing and would probably write a worse essay. The second person is very skilled at writing essays.

Whose feedback should you listen to? You should consider the feedback from the person who is better at writing, especially if they want to help you improve.

If someone is less skilled or criticizes you without wanting to help (or maybe because they are just mean), you can ignore their opinion.

People's role in your life is to help you, not hurt you, but it depends on whether you are making the correct distinction.

CARLA

"Why am I so different from everyone else?"

She wondered at age 20.

"Why can't anyone truly understand me, and why do I struggle to understand how people around me think?

In my family, it feels like we're living in two different worlds or at least different realities, even though we're on the same planet.

I say one thing, and everyone else seems to hear something completely different.

It's like I'm constantly battling just to communicate with people, and sometimes I feel so exhausted that I want to stop talking altogether."

Secret #10

Finding Your Identity

Finding one's identity is very important, especially when you're trying to overcome anxiety or depressive tendencies.

While we've been taught that we're all different and unique, and there's no set way to feel, think, act, or react, we have many similarities.

In the next four secrets, I'll focus on the ***four types of people in the world.*** I'll help you discover who you are and understand those around you.

This will help clear up any misunderstandings with others.

This information changed my life, and I believe it can change yours too.

The next 4 secrets will seem quite disruptive, but let's not forget that a mind has to be flexible and adaptable if we want to accept any growth and expansion into our lives.

So, let's get started!

THE CREATOR & THE PRINCESS

"I'm very sensitive and sometimes I have the impression that I am too emotional."

"I like art and dancing and I create new ideas which I don't always know how to put into reality.

I need somebody in my life who will protect me and take care of me.

A lot of times I find people who are hurting me and abusing me and then I get too sad and I don't know how to get out of these conditions."

"My biggest fear is being hurt and sometimes I even avoid socializing to protect my heart."

Secret #11

The Water Archetype

The most amazing archetype in human beings and the most complex at the emotional level is the water archetype.

Water holds the DNA of our entire world and everything from ideas and love. Most of the human body is made of water.

With the DNA of the entire world comes a lot of suffering, and it's easy for the water archetype to slip into a painful reality without knowing how to escape. The water archetype is usually an introvert.

But without the water archetype, there would be no love in the world and no new ideas to create everything we need.

THE MANAGER & THE MISTRESS

"There is so much passion in my heart."

"It's amazing because I have all this unlimited energy which sometimes, I don't even know how to use.

I am easily excited about everything, and I want to love and live and do everything, but sometimes I don't even know where to start, and other times I start one thing and I don't finish it because another thing comes up.

I am very well put together and I always consider myself and people around me as a priority, always trying to become better."

"When I am hurt, I become angry, and I use my energy in the wrong way."

Secret #12

The Fire Archetype

The fire archetype is absolutely amazing as it represents passion, the fuel of life, the blood in our veins that effortlessly makes us alive.

Without the fire in life, nothing will ever get done, no idea will have the passion to become something.

Sometimes the fire archetypes can exhaust others by having too much energy.

This archetype represents beauty, management, and sales, and it's usually an extrovert.

Heartbreak can affect them tremendously

If this happens, consider our relationship programs: *The 17 Costly Love Traps To Avoid*, *True Love Secrets*, and *Get Over Your Ex In 5 Days*

THE ENTREPRENEUR & THE QUEEN

"I like freedom and independence and I don't want anybody to tell me what to do."

"I like to experience new things, start businesses, and enjoy life and I don't like anything or anybody that holds me down.

Some consider me cold and even heartless, but the truth is that I know how to distinguish between my feelings and what I want to do. Plus, I prioritize myself fully.

When I am hurt, I don't show it because I don't believe that anybody cares."

"***Most people don't even realize that I can also get hurt, like everybody else.***"

Secret #13

The Air Archetype

Elegance, class, independence, freedom, and sometimes quite intimidating - this is the air archetype.

Without it, we will be stranded in ideas and passions, in feelings and emotions without accomplishing anything in life.

Their number one gift is to compartmentalize different emotions from what they have to do.

Though they get hurt like everybody else, they rarely stay hurt and nobody even knows about it because they know how to hide very well.

This is why they also accomplish a lot in their lives.

THE KING & THE MOTHER

"I like everything to be stable, and I rule my life by values, specifically family values."

"I choose jobs that have to do with teaching, army, farming, financing - foundational parts of a society.

I care about everybody around me, and I feel it's my job to protect them all.

I don't like overnight changes in my life and I don't really want to deal with suffering or with the process of getting out of suffering."

*"**I'm trying to ignore all these feelings because life moves on and things have to get done every day.**"*

Secret #14

The Earth Archetype

This archetype is a symbol of stability and results.

It's a final process of accomplishing an entire cycle of life that now needs to see the results and preserve them.

The Earth archetype is mature enough to understand what's important and what is not important in life.

Sometimes this archetype unconsciously carries suffering, with it and it's very opposed to even looking at its own suffering because it finds it irrelevant.

They hide suffering very well and they are also extremely stubborn.

Want to know more about archetypes?

Consider our program: *True Love Secrets*

CORINA

"The tendencies of anxiety and depression have persisted in my family for three generations, growing more intense and challenging with each passing one."

"It appears to be a pattern that keeps worsening, especially with the women in our family.

The question is: **why do these cycles repeat, and how can I help my family break free from this pattern?" asked Corina, 27, mother of 2.**

Understanding Tendencies to Anxiety & Depression

Tendencies towards anxiety and depression ***arise when an individual is unprepared to face life's challenges.*** These tendencies persist until they are properly addressed and can profoundly impact a person's entire life.

At the AntiDepression Institute, we witness numerous individuals trapped in these emotional and mental struggles.

The critical question arises:

How does one prepare effectively for life?

The answer lies in continuous personal growth and skill development, including mastering relationships with yourself and others, become emotional balanced and mentally strong.

GEORGE

"I have so many questions about life."

"Why do people you love not always love you back?

Why do people divorce?

Why do some people live in suffering, and others are happy?

How can you stop tendencies to anxiety and depression?

How can I be successful in life?

What does success look like?

How do I get along with people?

How can you not be heartbroken anymore?

What does self-love look like?

How can you stay away from narcissists?" asked George, age 24.

Consider our program: *Life Strategy With Results* for the answers to all of these questions.

Secret # 16

Finding The Right Answer

To find the right answer you need to ask the right question. Many people who have lived in suffering sometimes for generations ask the wrong questions. And then their expectations are wrong.

For example: 'Who is going to help me out of suffering?' ***Nobody can help you out of suffering except yourself.*** You just need to know how to do it and that is a skill that can be learned. Nobody can remove YOUR SUFFERING. The right question to ask would be: ***"What knowledge and life skills I need to get myself out of suffering?"***

Being attuned to the right questions takes courage and the readiness to receive an answer that you might not like.

DANIEL

*"**How did you get yourself immune to suffering?**"*

"Not only you, even your son. It doesn't matter what you guys are going through. You just always succeeded. There is no challenge you can't face and you always make it on the other side of," asked Daniel, 30, a member of my team.

It was very interesting because Daniel has observed my journey with cancer, and he was absolutely surprised of how I overcame my illness and how my son reacted to all of it.

It made me think: ***is it something that I have used unconsciously?***

And the answer was …YES!!!

Secret # 17

The F.I.N.A.L. Strategy to Overcome Any Challenge in Life

F - FORGET anything you know about your challenge. If you haven't solved your challenge yet, that means that everything you know is garbage;

I - Gather new INFORMATION about the problem, even if you don't believe in that information;

N - NAVIGATE the information, preferably with a mentor or somebody who has achieved the result you want to have;

A - APPLY the information. Knowing without the application gets you nowhere;

L - LEARN the LESSON of LIFE - every challenge occurs because a lesson of life hasn't been learned.

RINSE AND REPEAT FOR THE NEXT CHALLENGE IN LIFE

Staying in Touch with Us

YouTube channel **Ana Lennyr**

Podcast **My Challenge Is with Ana Lennyr**

For educators and community leaders, we offer lectures, webinars, workshops, and licensing for our programs.

Join our mission:

Save A Young Adult

www.saveayoungadult.com

POPULAR PROGRAMS at AntiDepression Institute

FOR TEENS (under 18) & PARENTS

Ending Young Adult Anxiety & Depression (90 min entire formula)

How Life Truly Works - 27 secrets by text message.

Most popular Licensing Program for high schools and colleges.

Parental Divorce FOR Young Adults - 7-week by text message

Teenager Transformational Formula - 9-week program to completely prepare your young adult for life.

www.antidepressioninstitute.com

POPULAR PROGRAMS at AntiDepression Institute

FOR LOVE & RELATIONSHIPS

The 17 Costly Love Traps to Avoid - text message program

True Love Secrets - spend 3 hours to learn everything about relationships

Fix Your Marriage in 49 days (text message program)

Get Over Your Ex in 5 days (signature program)

www.antidepressioninstitute.com

POPULAR PROGRAMS at AntiDepression Institute

FOR ENDING TENDENCIES TO ANXIETY & DEPRESSION

(For adults)

Secret Map to Overcome Anxiety & Depression (90 min entire formula Ana Lennyr uses)

How Life Truly Works - 27 secrets by text message.

The 17 Mind Traps Keeping Us in Suffering - text message program

Become Mentally Strong (Acquire Emotional Balance in 3 weeks)

Life Strategy with Results - Master the Game of Life in 7 weeks

www.antidepressioninstitute.com

Made in United States
Cleveland, OH
04 November 2026

47645297R00036